Sarah Daniel

AIR FRYER SNACK & SANDWICH
2 cookbooks in 1

EVERYDAY QUICK & EASY RECIPES FOR AIR FRYER LOVERS

Kensington Recipe Press

© 2021 Kensington Recipe Press - All rights reserved.

Photography Humbert Castillo
Graphic design Yuka Okuma
Editorial coordination Lizzie Martin

First edition March 2021

The following book is reproduced below to provide information that is as accurate and reliable as possible. Regardless, purchasing this book can be seen as consent because both the publisher and the author of this book are in no way experts on the topics discussed within. Any recommendations or suggestions that are made herein are for entertainment purposes only. Professionals should be consulted as needed before undertaking any of the actions endorsed herein. This declaration is deemed fair and valid by both the American Bar Association and the Committee of Publishers Association and is legally binding throughout the United States. Furthermore, the transmission, duplication, or reproduction of any of the following work, including specific information, will be considered an illegal act irrespective of if it is done electronically or in print. This extends to creating a secondary or tertiary copy of the work or a recorded document and can only express written consent from the publisher. All additional rights reserved. The information in the following pages is broadly considered a truthful and accurate account of facts. As such, any inattention, use, or misuse of the information in question by the reader will render any resulting actions solely under their purview. There are no scenarios in which the publisher or the original author of this work can be in any fashion deemed liable for any hardship or damages that may befall them after undertaking the information described herein. Additionally, the following pages' information is intended only for informational purposes and should thus be thought of as universal. As befitting its nature, it is presented without assurance regarding its prolonged validity or interim quality. Trademarks that are mentioned are done without written consent and can in no way be considered an endorsement from the trademark holder.

Table of Content

INTRODUCTION 8

SNACK & SANDWICH 9

- Prosciutto-Wrapped Parmesan Asparagus 11
- Bacon-Wrapped Jalapeño Poppers 12
- Spicy Buffalo Chicken Dip 14
- Bacon Jalapeño Cheese Bread 15
- Bacon Cheeseburger Dip 16
- Pork Rind Tortillas 18
- Mozzarella Sticks 19
- Bacon-Wrapped Onion Rings 21
- Mini Sweet Pepper Poppers 22
- Spicy Spinach Artichoke Dip 24
- Garlic Cheese Bread 26
- Loaded Roasted Broccoli 27
- Sausage-Stuffed Mushroom Caps 28
- Zucchini Parmesan Chips 30
- Kale Chips 31
- Italian Stuffed Sandwich 32
- Weekend Sandwich 34
- Peppery Turkey Sandwiches 35
- Italian Eggplant Sandwich 36
- Prosciutto Sandwich 38
- Roasted Bell Pepper Vegetable Salad 40
- Mushroom, Onion, and Feta Frittata 42
- Crispy Onion Rings 43
- Crisp Potato Wedges 45
- Roasted Heirloom Tomato with Baked Feta 46
- Garam Masala Beans 48
- Fried Pickles 49
- Roasted Eggplant 51
- Pita-Style Chips 53
- Flatbread 54
- Radish Chips 55
- Calzone 57
- Hash Brown Toast 58
- Roasted Garlic 59
- Spicy Cheese Meatballs 60
- Egg & Bacon Sandwich 61
- Ricotta Wraps & Spring Chicken 63
- Chicken Wrapped in Bacon 65

VEAL CLUB SANDWICH	66
PORK CLUB SANDWICH	68
PARMESAN HERB FOCACCIA	70
JICAMA FRIES	72
FRIED GREEN TOMATOES	74
CAULIFLOWER RELISH	75
BAKED ZUCCHINI FRIES	76
HOMEMADE TATER TOTS	78
SMOKED SAUSAGE MIX	79
MUSHROOM OATMEAL	81
CAULIFLOWER AVOCADO TOAST	82
GARLIC AND CHEESE BREAD ROLLS	83
WHEAT ANDSEED BREAD	84
DINNER ROLLS	86
ROASTED BELL PEPPER ROLLS	87
STUFFED PEPPERS	88
CREAMY CAULIFLOWER AND HAM BLEND	90
SPICY THAI BITES	91
ROLLED FLANKS	92
VEAL CLUB SANDWICH	94
EGGPLANT SANDWICH	96
SHRIMP SANDWICHES	97
MOZZARELLA SPINACH ROLLS	98
CRISPY EGGPLANT STRIPS	99
CRISP PARMESAN-POTATO BALLS	101
SWEET POTATO AND PARSNIPS CRISPS	103
POTATOES AU GRATIN	105
AIR FRIED KALE CHIPS	106
AIR-FRIED CALAMARI	108
CHEDDAR BACON CROQUETTES	109
MOROCCAN MEATBALLS WITH MINT YOGURT	110
TOMATO, CHEESE 'N BROCCOLI QUICHE	112
TASTY HASH BROWN	113
PORK BARBECUE SANDWICH	115
FISH CLUB SANDWICH	117
AIR FRYER SANDWICH	119
CHEESE SANDWICH	121
ONION FLOWERS	123
SWEET PEPPER AND POTATO STUFFED BREAD ROLLS	124
CRISPY PARSLEY AND GARLIC MUSHROOMS	125
CRISPY BROCCOLI TOTS	126
ROASTED WINTER VEGETABLES	128
CHEESY POLENTA	129
CAJUN SHRIMP	131

BROCCOLI ROUNDS WITH CHEESE	132
COCONUT CHICKEN BITES	133
CAULIFLOWER SNACK	135
SAUSAGE BALLS	136
CHICKEN DIP	137
SWEET POPCORN	138
SQUASH FRITTERS	140
CAULIFLOWER BUFFALO	141
FRIES AVOCADO	142
COCO MILK AND PAPRIKA DRUMSTICK	143

Introduction

Sarah Daniel is a passionate cookbook writer with over two decades of professional culinary expertise. Known for her culinary skills and high standard, she has combined her classic recipes tailored to use with the modern cooking appliance in her new cookbook series "The Complete Air Fryer Cookbook" for Kensington Recipe Press. She loves to employ innovations in cooking by keeping the traditional elements and richness.

We can always find the art of simplicity in her recipes, making her a step ahead of many innovative cooking methods. All of her books include self-tested recipes, and the pleasure of sharing exciting experiments is evident in most of her recipe works.

Popularly known as a "recipe development whiz" among her circle, she contributes recipes to several reputed magazines. She helps you discover something new and impressive. Beyond her books, she maintains a strong influence among her friends and family as an enthusiast of healthy eating and living.

Having spent considerable time writing the series "The Complete Air Fryer Cookbook", Sarah has carefully penned her research with super versatile meal ideas without compromising quality and nutritional values. Her approach to modern food tech is mind-blowing. This Cookbook Series is a pioneering endeavor blended with modern cooking with traditional values by focusing on healthy, balanced food. It is a reference series for people who love having healthy food.

Snack & Sandwich

Prosciutto-Wrapped Parmesan Asparagus

Ready in about 20 min | Servings 4 | Normal

Ingredients:

- 1-pound of asparagus
- 12 (0.5-ounce) slices of prosciutto
- 1 tablespoon of coconut oil, melted
- 2 teaspoons of lemon juice
- 1/8 teaspoon of red pepper flakes
- 1/3 cup of grated Parmesan cheese
- 2 tablespoons of salted butter, melted

Directions:

1. Place an asparagus spear onto a slice of prosciutto on a clean work surface.

2. Drizzle with the lemon juice and coconut oil. Sprinkle over asparagus with red pepper flakes and Parmesan. Roll prosciutto with a spear of asparagus. Put the basket into the Air Fryer.

3. Select bake mode the set the temperature to 375° F and set the timer for a further 10 minutes.

4. Before eating, sprinkle asparagus roll with butter.

Bacon-Wrapped Jalapeño Poppers

Ready in about 27 min | Servings 4 | Normal

Ingredients:

- 6 jalapeños (about 4" long each)
- 3-ounces of full-Fat: cream cheese
- 1/3 cup of shredded medium Cheddar cheese
- 1/4 teaspoon of garlic powder
- 12 slices sugar-free bacon

Directions:

1. Cut the tops off the jalapeños and slice lengthwise in two sections down the middle. Use a knife to cut the white membrane and pepper seeds with caution.

2. Place the cream cheese, Cheddar, and garlic powder in a large microwave-safe dish. Microwave, then stir for 30 seconds. Mixture the spoon of cheese with the jalapeños.

3. Wrap a strip of bacon around half of each jalapeño, shielding the pepper entirely. Put the basket into the Air Fryer.

4. Select bake mode the set the temperature to 400° F and change the timer for 12 minutes.

5. When the timer reaches 0, then press the cancel button

6. Switch the peppers halfway through the cycle of preparation. Serve warm.

Spicy Buffalo Chicken Dip

Ready in about 20 min | Servings 4 | Easy

Ingredients:

- 1 cup of cooked, diced chicken breast
- 8 ounces of full-Fat: cream cheese, softened
- 1/2 cup of buffalo sauce
- 1/3 cup of full-Fat: ranch dressing
- 1/3 cup of chopped pickled jalapeños
- 1 ½ cups of shredded medium Cheddar cheese, divided
- 2 scallions, sliced

Directions:

1. Place chicken into a large bowl. Add cream cheese, buffalo sauce, and ranch dressing. Stir until the spices are well mixed and mostly smooth. Fold in jalapeños and 1 cup Cheddar.

2. Pour the mixture into a 4-cup round baking dish and place the remaining Cheddar on top. Place the dish into the Air Fryer basket.

3. Adjust the temperature to 350°F and set the timer for 10 minutes.

4. When setting a cooking time less than 20 minutes, first set the cooking time to 20 minutes.

Then, turn the time/darkness control knob to the desired cooking time

5. When done, the top will be brown and bubbling. Top with sliced scallions. Serve warm.

Bacon Jalapeño Cheese Bread

Ready in about 25 min | Servings 2 | Yields 8 sticks | Normal

Ingredients:

- 2 cups of shredded mozzarella cheese
- ¼ cup of grated Parmesan cheese
- ¼ cup of chopped pickled jalapeños
- 2 large eggs
- 4 slices of sugar-free bacon, cooked and chopped

Directions:

1. Mix all ingredients in a large bowl. Cut a piece of parchment to fit your Air Fryer basket.

2. Dampen your hands with a bit of water and press out the mixture into a circle. You may need to separate this into two smaller cheese bread, depending on your fryer's size.

3. Place the parchment and cheese bread into the Air Fryer basket.

4. Adjust the temperature to 320°F and set the timer for 15 minutes.

5. Carefully flip the bread when 5 minutes remain.

6. When fully cooked, the top will be golden brown. Serve warm and enjoy!

Bacon Cheeseburger Dip

Ready in about 30 min | Servings 6 | Normal

Ingredients:

- 8 ounces of full-Fat: cream cheese
- 1/4 cup of full-Fat: mayonnaise
- 1/4 cup of full-Fat: sour cream
- 1/4 cup of chopped onion
- 1 teaspoon of garlic powder
- 1 tablespoon of Worcestershire sauce 1
- 1/4 cups of shredded medium Cheddar cheese, divided
- ½-pound of cooked 80/20 ground beef
- 6 slices of sugar-free bacon, cooked and crumbled
- 2 large of pickle spears, chopped.

Directions:

1. In a large microwave-safe bowl, place the cream cheese and microwave for 45 seconds. Stir in mayonnaise, sour cream, onion, powdered garlic, and one cup of Worcestershire Cheddar sauce. Add the bacon and the ground beef. Sprinkle over leftover Cheddar.

2. Place the bowl in 6 " and put it in the basket of the Air Fryer.

3. Select bake mode the set the temperature to 400° F and adjust the timer for 10 minutes.

4. When the top is golden, bubbling sprinkles the pickles over the dish and serves warm.

Pork Rind Tortillas

Ready in about 15 min | Servings 4 | Yields 4 tortillas| Easy

Ingredients:

- 1-ounce of pork rinds
- 3/4 cup of shredded mozzarella cheese
- 2 tablespoons of full-Fat: cream cheese
- 1 large egg

Directions:

1. Install pork rinds in a food processor and pulse until finely soiled.

2. Place the mozzarella in a large, safe microwave bowl. Break-in small pieces of the cream cheese and add to the bowl. Microwave for 30 seconds, or until both kinds of cheese are melted and easily stirred into a ball. To the cheese mixture, add the ground pork rinds and the egg.

3. Continue to stir till the mixture forms a ball. If it cools too much and hardens the cheese, then microwave for another 10 seconds.

4. Set the dough aside into four small balls. Place each dough ball between two parchment sheets, and roll into a 1/4 flat layer.

5. Place tortillas in a single layer Air Fryer basket; work in batches where necessary.

6. Set the temperature to 400° F and adjust the timer for 5 minutes.

7. When fully cooked, the tortillas will become crispy and firm. Serve immediately and enjoy!

Mozzarella Sticks

Ready in about 1 hour 10 min | Servings 3 | Yields 12 sticks | Normal

Ingredients:

- 6 (1-ounce) mozzarella string cheese sticks
- 1/2 cup of grated Parmesan cheese
- ½- an ounce of pork rinds, finely ground
- 1 teaspoon of dried parsley
- 2 large eggs

Directions:

1. Put the sticks of mozzarella on a cutting board and cut in half. Freeze to stand for 45 minutes or until solid. When freezing overnight, cut frozen sticks after 1 hour and put them in an airtight zip-top storage bag for future use.

2. Combine the Parmesan, ground pork rinds, and parsley in a large bowl.

3. Then whisk eggs in a medium bowl.

4. Brush a frozen mozzarella over beaten eggs, then coat in a Parmesan sauce. Repeat for unused sticks. Place the mozzarella sticks in the bowl of the Air Fryer.

5. Adjust the temperature to 400° F and set the timer to golden for 10 minutes.

6. Serve hot and enjoy!

Bacon-Wrapped Onion Rings

Ready in about 15 min | Servings 4 | Normal

Ingredients:

- 1 large onion, peeled
- 1 tablespoon of sriracha
- 8 slices of sugar-free bacon

Directions:

1. Slice of the ointment into 1/4"-thick slices. Take two slices of onion and tie the bacon around the rings. Repeat for the remaining onion and bacon.

2. Select bake mode the set the temperature to 350° F and change the timer for 10 minutes.

3. Use pliers to rotate the onion rings halfway through the cooking time. Bacon will be crispy when fully fried. Eat hot and enjoy it!

Mini Sweet Pepper Poppers

Ready in about 30 min | Servings 4 | Yields 16 halves| Normal

Ingredients:

- 8 mini sweet peppers
- 4 ounces of full-Fat: cream cheese, softened
- 4 slices of sugar-free bacon, cooked and crumbled
- 1/4 cup of shredded pepper jack cheese

Directions:

1. Cut the pepper tops and slice on half lengthwise each. To cut seeds and membranes using a small knife.
2. Put together the cream cheese, bacon, and pepper jack in a shallow tub.
3. In each sweet pepper, put 3 teaspoons of the mixture and press smoothly hard—place in basket fryer.
4. Select bake mode the set the temperature to 400° F, and set the timer for eight minutes.
5. When the timer reaches 0, then press the cancel button
6. Serve sweet and enjoy!

Spicy Spinach Artichoke Dip

Ready in about 20 min | Servings 6 | Easy

Ingredients:

- 10 ounces of frozen spinach, drained and thawed
- 1 (14-ounce) can of artichoke hearts, drained and chopped
- 1/4 cup of chopped pickled jalapeños
- 8 ounces of full-Fat: cream cheese, softened
- 1/4 cup of full-Fat: mayonnaise
- 1/4 cup of full-Fat: sour cream
- 1/2 teaspoon of garlic powder
- ¼ cup of grated Parmesan cheese
- 1 cup of shredded pepper jack cheese

Directions:

1. Combine the ingredients in a 4-cup baking dish. Put the basket into the Air Fryer.
2. Select bake mode the set the temperature to 320° F and change the timer for 10 minutes.
3. When the timer reaches 0, then press the cancel button
4. Start as orange, then bubble. Serve fresh and enjoy!

Garlic Cheese Bread

Ready in about 20 min | Servings 2 | Easy

Ingredients:

- 1 cup of shredded mozzarella cheese
- 1/4 cup of grated Parmesan cheese
- 1 large egg
- 1/2 teaspoon of garlic powder

Directions:

1. Mix the ingredients in a large bowl. Cut a piece of parchment to fit your basket with Air Fryer. Press the mixture on the parchment in a circle, and place it in the basket of the Air Fryer.

2. Select bake mode the set the temperature to 350° F and change the timer for 10 minutes.

3. When the timer reaches 0, then press the cancel button

4. Serve hot and enjoy!

Loaded Roasted Broccoli

Ready in about 20 min | Servings 2 | Easy

Ingredients:

- 3 cups of fresh broccoli florets
- 1 tablespoon of coconut oil
- 1/2 cup of shredded sharp Cheddar cheese
- 1/4 cup of full-Fat: sour cream
- 4slices of sugar-free bacon, cooked and crumbled
- 1 scallion, sliced

Directions:

1. Bring the broccoli into the Air Fryer tank and drizzle it with coconut oil.

2. Select bake mode the set the temperature to 350° F and change the timer 10 minutes longer.

3. Toss a basket for two or three times during the training or avoid burning spots.

4. Remove from the fryer as the broccoli continues to crisp at the top. Cover to garnish with melted cheese, sour cream, and crumbled slices of bacon and scallion.

Sausage-Stuffed Mushroom Caps

Ready in about 16 min | Servings 2 | Easy

Ingredients:

- 6 large portobello mushroom caps
- ½-pound of Italian sausage
- 1/4 cup of chopped onion
- 2 tablespoons of blanched finely ground almond flour
- ¼ cup of grated Parmesan cheese
- 1 teaspoon of minced fresh garlic

Directions:

1. Use a spoon to hollow each cap of the mushrooms, and save scrapings.

2. Brown the sausage in a medium saucepan over medium heat for around 10 minutes, or until fully cooked and no pink remains. Drain and then apply stored scrapings of mushroom, cabbage, almond flour, parmesan, and garlic. Fold ingredients gently together and continue cooking for a further minute, then remove from fire.

3. Scoop the mixture uniformly into mushroom caps and place the caps in a 6 round tub. Put the pan in the basket for the Air Fryer.

4. Select bake mode the set the temperature to 375° F, and set the timer for 8 minutes.

5. The tops will be browned and bubbling when done frying, and serve soft.

Zucchini Parmesan Chips

Ready in about 20 min | Servings 1 | Easy

Ingredients:

- 2 medium zucchinis
- 1-ounceof pork rinds
- 1/2 cup of grated Parmesan cheese
- 1 large egg

Directions:

1. Slice of zucchini in 1/4"-thick strips. Put 30 minutes between two layers of paper towels or a clean kitchen towel to eliminate any extra moisture.
2. Put pork rinds in a food processor and pulse until finely ground. Pour into a medium bowl and combine it with Parmesan.
3. Beat the egg in a shallow saucepan.
4. Dip the zucchini slices in the egg mixture and then in the pork rind mixture, cover as thoroughly as possible. Put each slice carefully in a single layer of the Air Fryer bowl, operating as required in batches.
5. Change the temperature to 320° F and set a 10-minute timer.
6. Flip chips halfway into time to cook. Serve hot and enjoy!

Kale Chips

Ready in about 10 min | Servings 4 | Easy

Ingredients:

- 4 cups of steamed kale
- 2 teaspoons of avocado oil
- 1/2 teaspoon of salt

Directions:

1. Swirl kale in avocado oil in a large tub, and sprinkle with salt. Place it in the basket of Air Fryer.
2. Change the temperature to 400° f and set a 5-minute timer.
3. When setting a cooking time less than 20 minutes, first set the cooking time to 20 minutes.

Then, turn the time/darkness control knob to the desired cooking time

4. When finished, the kale would be crispy. Serve forthwith.

Italian Stuffed Sandwich

Ready about in: 1 hr and 10 min| Serves 2|Easy

Ingredients

- ½ kg of flour medium strength.
- 10gr of fresh yeast
- 230 - 240ml of water.
- 60gr butter or oil.
- 1 teaspoon salt
- 1 teaspoon of sugar

Directions:

1. To do it manually: Dissolve the yeast in a little warm water.

2. Place the flour in the shape of a volcano in a large container. In the center place the oil, sugar, and salt. Move with a wooden spoon. Add the yeast and begin to integrate from the inside out. Now integrated, pass them to the work table.

3. Knead until a homogeneous mass is observed. It should not be stuck in the hands. Cover and let stand, about 1 hour.

4. Then spread the dough, trying to have a thickness of 2 to 6 millimeters.

5. Cut small rectangles and measure the center.

6. Place filling in the lower center part. Spread a little water on the edges with a thin brush to seal.

7. Cut the excess if you do it by machine, proceed according to the instructions.

8. Place in the Air Fryer for 10 - 12 minutes at 380° F.

They a Reserved up with creams to taste.

Weekend Sandwich

Ingredients

- 12 slices Sandwich bread
- 12 slices of turkey ham
- 6 slices of vegan cheese
- 1½ cups of grated yellow cheese
- 1 cup of milk cream
- 100 g of Butter
- Salt and pepper to taste

Directions:

1. First, spread a little butter on the bread slices. Place one of the loaves, two slices of ham, one of cheese and close.

2. Place in the Air Fryer and fry at 360° F for 2 minutes.

3. Meanwhile, in a bowl, mix the cheese, cream, salt, and pepper. Cover the sandwich with the mixture.

4. Fry at 340° F for 4 minutes until golden brown.

5. Serves and enjoy

Peppery Turkey Sandwiches

Read about in: 15 min| Servings: 4

Ingredients

- 7 ounces thinly sliced cracked black pepper-seasoned turkey breast
- 4 (3/4-ounce) slices Monterey Jack cheese with jalapeño peppers
- 3 (1-ounce) slices multigrain bread
- 4 tablespoons creamy mustard blend
- ½ cup mild banana pepper rings, drained

Directions:

1. Preheat broiler to your Air Fryer

2. Place bread slices on a baking sheet.

Toast bread on both sides

3. Spread 2 tablespoon mustard blend over each bread slice.

4. Arrange 2 ounces turkey on each bread slice. Place banana pepper rings evenly over turkey; top sandwiches with cheese slices.

5. Broil 5 minute or until cheese melts

Enjoy

Italian Eggplant Sandwich

Ready in about 26 min | Servings 2 | Easy

Ingredients:

- 1 eggplant, sliced
- 2 teaspoons of parsley, dried
- Salt and black pepper to the taste
- ½ cup of breadcrumbs
- ½ teaspoon of Italian seasoning
- ½ teaspoon of garlic powder
- ½ teaspoon of onion powder
- 2 tablespoons of milk
- 4 bread slices
- Cooking spray
- ½ cup of mayonnaise
- ¾ cup of tomato sauce
- 2 cups of mozzarella cheese, grated

Directions:

1. Season eggplant slices with salt and pepper, leave aside for 10 minutes and then pat dry them well.
2. In a bowl, mix parsley with breadcrumbs, Italian seasoning, onion and garlic powder, salt and black pepper, and stir.
3. In another bowl, mix milk with mayo and whisk well.
4. Brush eggplant slices with mayo mix, dip them in breadcrumbs, place them in your Air Fryer's basket, spray with cooking oil and cook them at 400° F for 15 flipping them after 8minutes.
5. Brush each bread slice with olive oil and arrange 2 on a working surface.

6. Add mozzarella and parmesan on each, add baked eggplant slices, spread tomato sauce and basil, and top with the other bread slices, greased side down.

7. Divide sandwiches between plates, cut them in halves, and serve. Enjoy!

Prosciutto Sandwich

Ready in about 15 min | Servings 1 | Normal

Ingredients:

- 2 bread slices
- 2 mozzarella slices
- 2 tomato slices
- 2 prosciutto slices
- 2 basil leaves
- 1 teaspoon of olive oil
- A pinch of salt and black pepper

Directions:

1. Arrange mozzarella and prosciutto on a bread slice.

2. Season with salt and pepper, place in your Air Fryer and cook at 400° F for 5 minutes.

3. Drizzle oil over prosciutto, add tomato and basil, cover with the other bread slice, cut the sandwich in half and serve.

Enjoy!

Roasted Bell Pepper Vegetable Salad

Ready in about 35 min | Servings 4 | Normal

Ingredients:

- 1½ ounces of yogurt
- 1 medium-sized red bell pepper
- 2ounces of rocket leaves
- 3 teaspoons of lime juice
- 1 romaine lettuce
- 1 ounce of olive oil
- Ground black pepper and salt to taste

Directions:

1. Heat your Air Fryer to 392° F and place the bell pepper into it. Roast for 10 minutes until a bit charred. Put the pepper in a bowl, cover, and leave for about 15minutes.

2. When the timer reaches 0, then press the cancel button

3. Divide the bell pepper into 4, remove skin and seeds and then slice the pepper into thin strips.

4. Mix the lime juice, olive oil, and yogurt thoroughly together in a bowl. Add the salt and pepper as required and stir.

5. Add the rocket leaves, lettuce, and pepper strips into the yogurt mixture and toss to mix.

Mushroom, Onion, and Feta Frittata

Ready in about 40 min | Servings 4 | Normal

Ingredients:

- 4 cups of button mushrooms, cleaned and cut thinly into ¼ inch
- 6 eggs
- 1 red onion, peeled and sliced thinly into ¼ an inch
- 6 tablespoons of feta cheese, crumbled
- 2 tablespoons of olive oil
- 1 pinch of salt

Directions:

1. Add olive oil to a sauté pan and swirl the onions and mushrooms around under medium heat until tender. Remove from heat and cool on a dry kitchen towel.

2. Select bake mode the set the temperature to preheat Air Fryer to 330°F. Whisk the eggs thoroughly in a mixing bowl and add a pinch of salt.

3. Coat the inside and bottom of an 8-in heat resistant baking dish lightly with spray. Pour the whisked eggs into the baking dish, add the onion and mushroom mixture and then add the cheese.

4. Place the dish in the cooking basket and cook 27 to 30 minutes in the Air Fryer or until an inserted knife in the frittata center comes out clean.

Crispy Onion Rings

Ready in about 35 min | Servings 2 | Easy

Ingredients:

- 1 big of sized onion, thinly sliced
- 8 ounces of milk
- 1 egg
- 6 ounces of breadcrumbs
- 1 teaspoon of baking powder
- 10 ounces of flour
- 1 teaspoon of salt

Directions:

1. Heat your Air Fryer to 360° F for 10 minutes.
2. Detach the onion slices to separate rings.
3. Mix the baking powder, flour, and salt in a bowl.
4. Put the onion rings into the flour mixture to coat them. Beat the egg and the milk and stir into the flour to form a batter. Dip the flour-coated rings in the batter.
5. Put the bread crumbs in a small tray, place the onion rings in it, and ensure all sides are well coated.
6. Place the rings in the fryer basket and Air Fry for 10 minutes until crisp. Enjoy!

Crisp Potato Wedges

Ready in about 40 min | Servings 4 | Normal

Ingredients:

- 3 teaspoons of olive oil
- 2 big potatoes
- ¼ cup of sweet chili sauce
- ¼ cup of sour cream

Directions:

1. Slice the potatoes lengthwise to create a wedge shape.
2. Select bake mode the set the temperature to Air Fryer to 356° F.
3. Place the wedges in a bowl and add the oil. Toss lightly until the potatoes are fully coated with the oil.
4. Put into the cooking basket with the skin side facing down and cook for about 15 minutes. Toss, then cook for an other 10 minutes until golden brown.
5. Best served while warm with chili source and sour cream.

Roasted Heirloom Tomato with Baked Feta

Ready in about 35 min | Servings 4 | Easy

Ingredients:

For the Tomato:

- 2 heirloom tomatoes, sliced thickly into ½ inch circular slices
- 1 8-ounce of feta cheese, sliced thickly into ½ inch circular slices
- ½ cup of red onions, sliced thinly
- 1 pinch of salt
- 1 tablespoon of olive oil

For the Basil Pesto:

- ½ cup of basil, chopped roughly
- ½ cup of parsley, roughly chopped
- 3 tablespoons of pine nuts, toasted
- ½ cup of parmesan cheese, grated
- 1 garlic clove
- 1 pinch of salt
- ½ cup of olive oil

Directions:

1. Begin by making the pesto. To do this, combine garlic, parmesan, parsley, toasted pine nuts, basil, and salt in a food processor.

2. Turn it on and gradually add the olive oil to incorporate into the pesto. Once done, store and put in the refrigerator until ready to use.

3. Preheat the Air Fryer to 390° F. Pat dry tomato with a paper towel. Spread a tablespoon of the pesto on top of each slice of tomato and top with the feta. Add 1 tablespoon of olive oil to the red onions and toss; place on top of the feta.

4. Now place the feta / tomatoes into the cooking basket and cook until the feta is brownish and starts to soften or 12 to 14 minutes.

5. Add a pinch of salt and 1 spoonful of basil pesto. Serve and enjoy.

Garam Masala Beans

Ready in about 17 min | Servings 4 | Easy

Ingredients:

- 9-ounce of Beans
- 2 Eggs
- 1/2 cup of breadcrumbs
- 1/2 cup of flour
- 1/2 teaspoon of garam masala
- 2 teaspoon of chili powder
- Olive Oil
- Salt to taste

Directions:

1. Preheat the Air Fryer at 350°F. Combine chili powder, garam masala, flour, and salt in a bowl, mixing well. Beat the eggs and set one side.
2. Pour the bread crumbs on a separate plate, then coat the beans with the flour mixture. Now dip beans into the egg mixture and next, into the bread crumbs. Do this with all the beans.
3. Place the beans into the Air Fryer tray and cook for 4 minutes. Open and coat the beans with oil and cook once more for another 3 minutes.
Serve warm and enjoy!

Fried Pickles

Ready in about 15 min | Servings 4 | Easy

Ingredients:

- 1 tablespoon of coconut flour
- 1/3 cup of blanched finely ground almond flour
- 1 teaspoon of chili powder
- 1/4 teaspoon of garlic powder
- 1 large egg
- 1 cup of sliced pickles

Directions:

1. In a medium dish, mix the coconut flour, almond meal, chili powder, and garlic powder.
2. Whisk the egg in a tiny mug.
3. Pat with a paper towel on each pickle and dunk in the egg. Then dredge in the mixture with flour. Put the pickles in the bowl for Air Fryer.
4. Switch to 400° F and set the timer for 5 minutes.
5. Flip the pickles halfway through the duration of preparation.

Roasted Eggplant

Ready in about 30 min | Servings 4 | Easy

Ingredients:

- 1 large eggplant
- 2 tablespoons of olive oil
- 1/4 teaspoon of salt
- 1/2 teaspoon of garlic powder

Directions:

1. Cut eggplant top and bottom. Break the eggplant into small thick strips.

2. Spray the slices with the olive oil and sprinkle with salt and garlic powder. Put the pieces of the eggplant in the container of your Air Fryer.

3 Select bake mode the set the temperature to 390° F and change the timer for 15 minutes.

4. When the timer reaches 0, then press the cancel button

5. Serve forthwith and enjoy!

Pita-Style Chips

Ready in about 15 min | Servings 4 | Easy

Ingredients:

- 1 cup of shredded mozzarella cheese
- ¼ cup of blanched finely ground almond flour
- ½ teaspoon ground black pepper
- ½ teaspoon dried basil
- ½ cup olive oil
- 1 large egg

Directions:

1. Put the mozzarella in a large microwave and microwave bowl for 30 seconds or until it has melted. Add remaining ingredients and stir to a smooth finish; the dough quickly shapes into a ball. Microwave for 15 seconds if the dough is too rough.
2. Roll the dough out into a wide rectangle between two sheets of parchment and then use a knife to cut chips in a triangle shape. Place the chips in the basket for Air Fryer.
3. Select bake mode the set the temperature to 400° F and set the timer for 5 minutes.
4. When finished, the chips would be golden in color and solid. They'll get much firmer as they cool off.

Flatbread

Ready in about 11 min | Servings 2 | Easy

Ingredients:

- 1 cup of shredded mozzarella cheese
- 1/4 cup of blanched finely ground almond flour
- 1 ounce of full-Fat: cream cheese, softened

Directions:

1. Melt mozzarella in a big, microwave-safe bowl for 30 seconds. Incorporate the almond flour until creamy, then add cream cheese. Continue to mix until the dough shapes, kneading it gently with wet hands if necessary.

2. Break the dough into two parts and stretch out between two parchments to 1/4" thickness. Cut another slice of parchment to match your Air Fryer tray.

3. Put a piece of flatbread on your parchment and in the Air Fryer and work in two lots if necessary.

4. Select bake mode the set the temperature to 320° F, and set the timer for 7 minutes.

5. Turn the flat-bread halfway through the cooking time. Serve hot.

Radish Chips

Ready in about 15 min | Servings 4 | Easy

Ingredients:

- 2 cups of water
- 1-pound of radishes
- 1/4 teaspoon of onion powder
- 1/4 teaspoon of paprika
- 1/2 teaspoon of garlic powder
- 2 tablespoons of coconut oil, melted

Directions:

1. Put water in a medium saucepan over a stovetop and bring to a boil.
2. Cut the top and bottom of each radish, then slice each radish thinly and evenly with a mandolin. For this stage, you might also be using the slicing blade in the food processor.
3. Place the slices of radish in boiling water for 5 minutes, or until they are translucent. Remove from the bath and put in a clean kitchen towel to absorb extra humidity.
4. Put in a big bowl the radish chips with the remaining one's ingredients and seasoning until thoroughly covered in grease. Place radish chips inside the basket of the Air Fryer.
5. Change to 320° F and set the timer for 5 minutes.
6. Shake a basket during the cooking process, two to three times. Enjoy!

Calzone

Ready in about 30 min | Servings 4 | Normal

Ingredients:

- 1 ½ cups of shredded mozzarella cheese
- ½ cup of blanched finely ground almond flour
- 1 ounce of full-Fat: cream cheese
- 1 large whole egg
- 4 large eggs, scrambled
- ½ pound cooked breakfast sausage, crumbled
- 8 tablespoons of shredded mild Cheddar cheese

Directions:

1. In a large microwave-safe bowl, add mozzarella, almond flour, and cream cheese—microwave for 1 minute. Stir until the mixture is smooth and forms a ball. Add the egg and stir until dough forms.

2. Place dough between two sheets of parchment and roll out to ¼ " thickness. Cut the dough into four rectangles.

3. Mix scrambled eggs and cooked sausage together in a large bowl. Divide the mixture evenly among each dough piece, placing it on the lower half of the rectangle. Sprinkle each with 2 tablespoons Cheddar.

4. Fold over the rectangle to cover the egg and meat mixture. Pinch, roll, or use a wet fork to close the edges completely.

5. Cut a parchment piece to fit your Air Fryer basket and place the calzones onto the parchment. Place parchment into the Air Fryer basket.

6. Adjust the temperature to 380° F and set the timer for 15 minutes.

7. Flip the calzones halfway through the cooking time. When done, calzones should be golden in color. Serve immediately.

Enjoy!

Hash Brown Toast

Ready in about 17 min | Serves 4 | Normal

Ingredients:

- 4 hash brown patties, frozen
- 1 tablespoon olive oil
- ¼ cup cherry tomatoes, chopped
- 3 tablespoons mozzarella cheese, shredded
- 2 tablespoons Parmesan cheese, grated
- 1 tablespoon balsamic vinegar
- 1 tablespoon basil, chopped

Directions:

1. Place hash brown patties in your Air Fryer, pour oil over them and cook at 400° F for 7 minutes.

2. In a bowl, mix tomatoes with mozzarella, parmesan, vinegar and basil and toss well.

3. Divide hash brown patties among plates, top each with tomato mixture and serve.

Enjoy.

Roasted Garlic

Ready in about 20 min | Servings 1 | Easy

Ingredients:

- 1 medium head of garlic
- 2 teaspoons of avocado oil

Directions:

1. Strip any excess peel hanging from the garlic still cover the cloves. Shutdown
1/4 of the garlic handle, with clove tips visible.

2. Avocado oil spray. Place the garlic head in a small sheet of aluminum foil, and enclose it completely. Place it in the basket for Air Fryer.

3. Set the temperature to 400° F and change the timer for 20 minutes. If your garlic head is a little smaller, take 15 minutes to check it out.

4. Ail should be golden brown and very fluffy when finished.

5. Cloves should pop out to eat and be scattered or sliced quickly. In the refrigerator, lock in an airtight jar for up to 5 days. You can also freeze individual cloves on a baking sheet, then lock them together until frozen in a freezer-safe storage jar.

Spicy Cheese Meatballs

Ready about in: 15 min|Serves 4|Easy

Ingredients

- 600g Cheddar cheese in cubes
- 240g Clean Chilies
- 2 eggs beaten with salt
- Doritos
- Olive oil

Directions:

1. In a processor, add half of the Chilies and cheese until you have a paste.
2. Cut the rest of the chilies finely and incorporate them into the dough.
3. Knead until integrating all the chilies. Grind the Doritos to make a powder. Assemble the meatballs.
4. Pass them by egg and Doritos. Brush them with olive oil and add them to the Air Fryer.
5. Fry at 360° F for 5 to 8 minutes.
6. When the timer reaches 0, then press the cancel button

Serve up with yogurt sauce, alone or with pink sauce

Egg & Bacon Sandwich

- Ready in about 12 min | Servings 1 | Easy
- Ingredients:
- 2 Bacon Slices
- 1 Egg
- 1 English muffin
- Salt and pepper to the taste

Directions:

1. Beat the egg into a soufflé cup and add salt and pepper to taste.

2 Select bake mode the set the temperature to Air Fryer to 390°F and place the soufflé cup, English muffin, and bacon into the tray.

3. When the timer reaches 0, then press the cancel button

4. Cook all the ingredients for 6-10 minutes.

Assemble the sandwich and Enjoy!

Ricotta Wraps & Spring Chicken

Ready about in 20 min| Servings: 12

Ingredients

- 2 large-sized chicken breasts, cooked and shredded
- ⅓ tablespoons sea salt
- ¼ tablespoons ground black pepper, or more to taste
- 2 spring onions, chopped
- ¼ cup soy sauce
- 1 tablespoons molasses
- 1 tablespoons rice vinegar
- 10 ounces Ricotta cheese
- 1 tablespoons grated fresh ginger
- 50 wonton wrappers

Directions:

1. In a bowl, combine all of the ingredients, minus the wonton wrappers.

2. Unroll the wrappers and spritz with cooking spray.

3. Fill each of the wonton wrappers with equal amounts of the mixture.

4. Dampen the edges with a little water as an adhesive and roll up the wrappers, fully enclosing the filling.

5. Cook the rolls in the Air Fryer for 5 minutes at 375°F. You will need to do this step in batches.

Serve with your preferred sauce.

Chicken Wrapped in Bacon

Ready about in : 25 min | Servings: 6 |

Ingredients

- 6 rashers unsmoked back bacon
- 1 small chicken breast
- 1 tablespoons garlic soft cheese

Directions:

1. Cut the chicken breast into six bite-sized pieces.

2. Spread the soft cheese across one side of each slice of bacon.

3. Put the chicken on top of the cheese and wrap the bacon around it, holding it in place with a toothpick.

4. Transfer the wrapped chicken pieces to the Air Fryer and cook for 15 minutes at 350° F.

When the timer reaches 0, then press the cancel button

5. Serve and Enjoy

Veal Club Sandwich

Ready in about 30 min | Servings 2 | Normal

Ingredients:

- 2 slices of white bread
- 1 tablespoons of softened butter
- ½ libbre of cubed veal
- 1 small capsicum
- For Barbeque Sauce:
- ¼ tablespoons of Worcestershire sauce
- ½ tablespoons of olive oil
- ½ flake garlic crushed
- ¼ cup of chopped onion
- ¼ tablespoons of mustard powder
- ½ tablespoons of sugar
- ¼ tablespoons of red chili sauce

Directions:

1. Take the bread slices and cut the rims. Still cut horizontally on the strips. Heat the sauce ingredients and wait before sauce thickens. Now apply the veal to the sauce, and whisk until the flavors are obtained.
2. Whisk the capsicum and scrape off the flesh. The capsicum is sliced into strips. Mix the ingredients, and add them to the slices of bread.
3. Select bake mode the set the temperature to preheat the Air Fryer to 300°F for 5 minutes. Open the Fryer's basket and put the cooked sandwiches in it, ensuring that no two sandwiches meet each other.

4. Hold the Air Fryer at about 15 minutes now at 250° F. Switch the sandwiches to cook both slices in between the cooking process. Serve the strawberry ketchup or mint chutney sandwiches.

5. Enjoy

Pork Club Sandwich

Ready in about 30 min | Servings 2 | Normal

Ingredients:

- 2 slices of white bread
- 1 tablespoons of softened butter
- ½ lb. of cut pork (get the meat cut into cubes)
- 1 small capsicum
- <u>For Barbeque Sauce:</u>
- ¼ tablespoons of Worcestershire sauce
- ½ tablespoons of olive oil
- ½ flake garlic crushed
- ¼ cup chopped onion
- ¼ tablespoons of mustard powder
- ½ tablespoons of sugar
- ¼ tablespoons of red chili sauce
- 1 tablespoons of tomato ketchup
- ½ cup of water.
- A pinch of salt and black pepper to the taste

Directions:

1. Take the bread slices and cut the rims. Still cut horizontally on the strips. Heat the sauce ingredients and wait before the sauce thickens. Now apply the pork to the sauce and whisk before the flavors are acquired.
2. Whisk the capsicum and scrape off the flesh. The capsicum is sliced into strips. Mix the ingredients, and add them to the slices of bread.
3. Select bake mode the set the temperature to preheat the Air Fryer to 300°F for 5 minutes.

3. Open the Fryer's basket and put the cooked sandwiches in it, ensuring that no two sandwiches meet each other. Hold the fryer at about 15 minutes now at 250°.

4. Switch the sandwiches to cook both slices in between the cooking process. Serve the strawberry ketchup or mint chutney sandwiches.

Parmesan Herb Focaccia

Ready in about 20 min | Servings 6 | Normal

Ingredients:

- 1 cup of shredded mozzarella cheese
- 1 ounce of full-Fat: cream cheese
- 1 cup of blanched finely ground almond flour
- 1/4 cup of ground golden flaxseed
- 1/4 cup of grated Parmesan cheese
- 1/2 teaspoon of baking soda
- 2 large eggs
- 1/2 teaspoon of garlic powder
- 1/4 teaspoon of dried basil
- 1/4 teaspoon of dried rosemary
- 2 tablespoons of salted butter, melted and divided

Directions:

1. In a large microwave-safe bowl and microwave, put the mozzarella, cream cheese, and almond flour for 1 minute. Add parmesan, flaxseed, and baking soda, and swirl until the ball becomes flat. If the mixture cools too soon, so blending is going to be difficult. Return to the microwave to rewarm for 10–15 seconds if required.

2. Substitute chickens. You may need to use your hands to integrate them to the full. Only keep cooking, and incorporate them into the batter.

3. Mix the garlic powdered dough with the basil and rosemary and knead into the dough. Grease 1 tablespoon melted butter into a round baking pan. Place the dough in the pan equally. Put the pan in the basket for the Air Fryer.

4. Select bake mode the set the temperature to 400° F and change the timer for 10 minutes.

5. Cover with foil at 7 minutes if the bread starts getting too dark.

6. Remove and cool for at least 30 minutes, mix with remaining butter and serve.

Jicama Fries

Ready in about 30 min | Servings 4 | Easy

Ingredients:

- 1 small jicama, peeled
- 3/4 teaspoon of chili powder
- 1/4 teaspoon of garlic powder
- 1/4 teaspoon of onion powder
- 1/4 teaspoon of ground black pepper

Directions:

1. Break the jicama into 1" cubes. Put in a wide bowl and mix with the coconut oil until seasoned. Sprinkle with the pepper and salt. Put the pepper and onion in the Air Fryer container.
2. Change the temperature to 400° F and set a 10-minute timer.
3. When the timer reaches 0, then press the cancel button
4. When frying, shake two to three times. Jicama will be soft and dark around the edges and serve immediately.

Fried Green Tomatoes

Ready in about 17 min | Servings 4 | Easy

Ingredients:

- 2 medium green tomatoes
- 1 large egg
- 1/4 cup of blanched finely ground almond flour
- 1/3 cup of grated Parmesan cheese

Directions:

1. Slice the tomatoes into 1/2" thick strips. Whisk the egg in a medium bowl. Mix the almond flour and Parmesan in a big bowl.

2. Dip each slice of tomato into the egg, then dredge in the mixture of almond flour, and put the slices in the Air Fryer basket.

3. Select bake mode the set the temperature to 400° F, and set the timer for 7 minutes.

4. When the timer reaches 0, then press the cancel button

5. Turn the slices halfway through the duration of preparation. Serve immediately.

Cauliflower Relish

Ready in about 22 min | Servings 4 | Easy

Ingredients:

- 1 head of cauliflower, cut into small florets
- 2 teaspoons of garlic powder
- 1 tablespoon of butter, melted
- 1/2 cup of chili sauce
- Olive oil
- Pinch salt and pepper

Directions:

1. In a bowl, pour oil over cauliflower florets to lightly cover—season with salt, pepper, and garlic powder and toss.

2. Place into Air Fryer at 350°F for 14 minutes and remove. Add together the chili sauce and melted butter, then pour over the florets to coat well.

3. Return to the Air Fryer and cook for 3 to 4 minutes longer.

Enjoy!

Baked Zucchini Fries

Ready in about 22 min | Servings 4 | Easy

Ingredients:

- 3 medium zucchinis, sliced lengthwise
- 1/2 cup of seasoned breadcrumbs
- 2 egg, the white part
- 1/4 teaspoon of garlic powder
- 2 tablespoons of parmesan cheese, grated
- Salt and pepper to taste

Directions

1. Beat egg whites in a bowl and season with salt and pepper.

2. In a separate bowl, combine garlic powder, breadcrumbs, and cheese.

3. Dip the zucchini sticks into the egg, bread crumb, and cheese mixture one after the other, then place on a single layer in the Air Fryer tray.

4. Coat lightly with cooking spray and bake for about 15 minutes at 390° F until golden brown.

5. Serve with a marinara sauce for dipping.

Homemade Tater Tots

Ready in about 30 min | Servings 2 | Easy

Ingredients:

- 1 medium-sized russet potato, chopped
- 1 teaspoon of ground onion
- 1 teaspoon of vegetable oil
- ½ teaspoon of ground black pepper
- Salt to taste

Directions:

1. Boil the potatoes until a bit more than al dente. Drain off water, add onions, oil, and pepper to it, and mash.

2. Select bake mode the set the temperature to preheat the Air Fryer to 379° F.

3. Mold the mash potatoes into tater tots. Place into the Air Fryer and bake for8 minutes. Shake the tots and bake for 5 minutes longer.

Smoked Sausage Mix

Ready in about 40 mins | Serving 4 | Easy

Ingredients:

- 1 and ½ pounds of smoked sausage, chopped and browned
- A pinch of salt and black pepper
- 1 and ½ cups of grits
- 4 and ½ cups of water
- 16 ounces of cheddar cheese, shredded
- 1 cup of milk
- ¼ teaspoon of garlic powder
- 1 and ½ teaspoons of thyme, chopped
- Cooking spray
- 4 eggs, whisked

Directions:

1. Put the water in a kettle, over medium heat, bring to a boil, add grits, stir, cover, simmer for 5 minutes and take off the heat.
2. Remove the cheese, whisk until it melts, then blend well with the butter, thyme, salt, pepper, garlic powder, and eggs.
3. Warm up the Air Fryer at 300° F, steam spray with grease, and add pork sausage.
4. Stir in grits, scatter and simmer for 25 minutes.
5. Serve for breakfast and split between dishes.

Enjoy!

Mushroom Oatmeal

Ready in about 30 min | Servings 4 | Normal

Ingredients:

- 1 small yellow onion, chopped
- 1 cup of steel-cut oats
- 2 garlic cloves, minced
- 2 tablespoons of butter
- ½ cup of water
- 14 ounces of canned chicken stock
- 3 thyme springs, chopped
- 2 tablespoons of extra virgin olive oil
- ½ cup of gouda cheese, grated
- 8 ounces of mushroom, sliced
- Salt and black pepper to the taste

Directions:

1. Heat a pan over medium heat that suits your Air Fryer with the butter, add onions and garlic, stir and cook for 4 minutes.
2. Attach oats, sugar, salt, pepper, stock, and thyme, stir, place in the Air Fryer and cook for 16 minutes at 360° F.
3. In the meantime, prepare a skillet over medium heat with the olive oil, add mushrooms, cook them for 3 minutes, add oatmeal and cheese, whisk, divide into bowls and serve.

Enjoy!

Cauliflower Avocado Toast

Ready in about 23 min | Servings 2 | Normal

Ingredients:

- 1 (12-ounce) steamer bag cauliflower
- 1 large egg
- 1/2 cup of shredded mozzarella cheese
- 1 ripe medium avocado
- 1/2 teaspoon of garlic powder
- 1/4 teaspoon of ground black pepper

Directions:

1. Whisk the eggs and the cream together in a medium bowl. Pour into a round baking dish with 4 cups.

2. Apply and combine the cauliflower, then finish with Cheddar. Drop the dish into the tray for the Air Fryer.

3. Set the temperature to 320° F and change the timer for 20 minutes.

4. When fully cooked, the eggs are firm, and the cheese is browned. Cut into 4 bits.

5. Dice the avocado and uniformly break into bits. Using 2 tablespoons of sour cream, sliced scallions, and crumbled bacon to cover each portion. Enjoy!

Garlic and Cheese Bread Rolls

Ready in about 15 min | Servings 2 | Normal

Ingredients:

8 tablespoons of grated cheese

6 teaspoons of melted butter

Garlic bread spice mix

2 bread rolls

Directions:

1. Slice the bread rolls from the top in a crisscross pattern but not cut through at the bottom.

2. Put all the cheese into the slits and brush the tops of the bread rolls with melted butter. Sprinkle the garlic mix on the rolls.

3. Select bake mode the set the temperature to heat the Air Fryer to 350° F. Place the rolls into the basket and cook until cheese is melted for about 5 minutes.

4. When the timer reaches 0, then press the cancel button

Enjoy!

Wheat andSeed Bread

Ready in about 1 hour 28 min | Servings 4 | Normal

Ingredients:

- 3½ ounces of flour
- 1 teaspoon of yeast
- 1 teaspoon of salt
- 3½ ounces of wheat flour
- ¼ cup of pumpkin seeds

Directions:

1. Mix the wheat flour, yeast, salt, seeds, and plain flour in a large bowl. Stir in ¾ cup of lukewarm water, and keep stirring until dough becomes soft.

2. Knead for another 5 minutes until the dough becomes elastic and smooth. Mold into a ball and cover with a plastic bag. Set aside for 30 minutes for it to rise.

3. Select bake mode the set the temperature to heat your Air Fryer to 392°F.

4. Transfer the dough into a small pizza pan and place it in the Air Fryer. Bake for 18 minutes until golden. Remove and place on a wire rack to cool. Enjoy!

Dinner Rolls

Ready in about 22 min | Servings 4 | Easy

Ingredients:

- 1 cup of shredded mozzarella cheese
- 1 ounce of full-Fat: cream cheese
- 1 cup of blanched finely ground almond flour
- 1/4 cup of ground flaxseed
- ½ teaspoon of baking powder
- 1 large egg

Directions:

1. In a large microwave-safe dish, put the mozzarella, cream cheese, and almond flour -1-minute Microwave. Mix until smooth.
2. Substitute the flaxseed, baking powder, and egg until smooth and fully mixed. If it gets too rigid, pulse another 15 seconds.
3. Set the dough apart into six pieces and roll it into balls. Place the balls in the basket for Air Fryer.
4. Switch to 320° F and set the timer for 12 minutes.
5. Cause the rolls to thoroughly cool before serving.

Roasted Bell Pepper Rolls

Ready in about 20 min | Servings 6 | Normal

Ingredients:

- 1 yellow bell pepper, halved
- 1 orange bell pepper, halved
- Salt and black pepper to the taste
- 4 ounces of feta cheese, crumbled
- 1 green onion, chopped
- 2 tablespoons of oregano, chopped

Directions:

1. Mix the cheese and the onion, oregano, salt, and pepper in a cup and whisk well.
2. Place halves of bell pepper in the basket of your Air Fryer, cook for 10 minutes at 400° F, move to a cutting board, cool down, and peel.
3. When the timer reaches 0, then press the cancel button
4. Break the cheese mixture into each half of the bell pepper, slice, secure with toothpicks, place on a plate, and serve as an appetizer.

Enjoy!

Stuffed Peppers

Ready in about 18 min | Servings 8 | Normal

Ingredients:

- 8 small bell peppers, tops cut off and seeds removed
- 1 tablespoon of olive oil
- Salt and black pepper to the taste
- 3.5 ounces of goat cheese, cut into 8 pieces

Directions:

1. In a cup, add salt and pepper to the cheese and oil, and mix to cover.

2. Fill each pepper with goat cheese, put them in the basket of your Air Fryer, cook for 8 minutes at 400° F, arrange them on a platter and serve as an appetizer.

Enjoy!

Creamy Cauliflower and Ham Blend

Ready in about 2hr 10 min | Servings 6 | Difficult

Ingredients:

- 8 grated ounces of cheddar cheese
- 4 ounces of ham, cubed cups
- 14 ounces of chicken
- 1/2 tablespoon of crushed garlic
- 1/2 tablespoon of ground onion
- Salt and black pepper, to satisfy
- 4 cloves of garlic, diced
- 1/4 cup of milk
- 16 ounces of cauliflower blossoms

Directions:

1. Blend ham and stock cheese in a pot that suits your Air Fryer. Mix cauliflower, powdered garlic, onion powder, milk, chili pepper, lime and stir in heavy cream, put the fryer in the air, and cook 300° F for 30 minutes.

2. When the timer reaches 0, then press the cancel button

3. Split in and place in pots.

Enjoy!

Spicy Thai Bites

Ready in about 20 min | Servings 4 | Normal

Ingredients:

- 400 g of minced pork
- 1 sizeable onion
- 1 tablespoon of garlic puree
- 1 tablespoon of soy sauce
- 1 tablespoons of Worcestersauce
- 1 tablespoon of Thai red curry pasta
- 1/2 (rind and juice) lime
- 1 tablespoon of blended spice
- 1 tablespoon of Chinese spice
- 1 tablespoon of coriander
- Salt and pepper

Directions:

1. In a tub, put all the ingredients and blend well.
2. Put them in the Air Fryer and form them into balls.
3. Cook for 15 minutes at a heat of 365° F in the Air Fryer.
4. When setting a cooking time less than 20 minutes, first set the cooking time to 20 minutes.

Then, turn the time/darkness control knob to the desired cooking time

5 Enjoy

Rolled Flanks

Ready in about 30 min | Servings 4 | Normal

Ingredients:

- 1 8-ounce of crescent rolls can
- 1 12-ounce of package cocktail franks

Directions:

1. Drain the cocktail franks and pat dry on paper towels. Cut the dough into rectangular-shaped strips, about 1-inch x 1.5-inch.
2. Roll the cut strips around the franks, ensuring that the ends can be seen. Make them firm by placing them in the freezer for 5 minutes.
3. Preheat the Air Fryer to 330° F. Take the franks out from the freezer and place it in the cooking basket—Cook for 6 to8 minutes.
4. Reset the temperature to 390° F and cook again for 3 minutes. Once it is golden brown, remove, serve, and enjoy.

Veal Club Sandwich

Ready in about 30 min | Servings 4 | Normal

Ingredients:

- Two slices of whole white bread
- 1 tablespoons of smooth butter
- 1/2 pounds of cubed veal
- 1 small capsicum

For barbeque sauce:

- 1/4 tablespoons Worcestershire
- 1/2 crushed garlic flake
- 1/4 cup of ointment
- 1/4 tablespoons powder mustard
- 1/2 tablespoons sugar
- 1/4 tablespoons hot sauce with chili
- 1 1/2 cup of water

Directions:

1. Take the bread slices and cut the rims. Now horizontally cut the slices.
2. Heat the sauce ingredients and wait before sauce thickens. Now bring in the veal to the sauce until the flavors are obtained—roast in the capsicum and peel off the skin. The capsicum is sliced into strips. Combine products, and apply it to slices of bread.
3. Select bake mode the set the temperature to preheat the Air Fryer to 300° F for five minutes. Open the Fryer basket and put the sandwiches prepared in it so that no two Sandwiches bump into each other.
4. Now keep the fryer at 250° F for 15 minutes. Switch the sandwiches in-between the cooking process both slices. Serve the sandwiches with spicy ketchup or mint chutney.

Eggplant Sandwich

Ingredients

- Bread of preference
- 1 small Eggplants, halved and sliced
- 1 tablespoons olive oil
- 2 French sandwinch rolls
- 1\2 cup crumbled feta cheese
- Aioli or other sauce to taste
- Parsley cut

Directions:

1. Preheat your oven's broiler.

2. Cut the eggplants into cubes. In the mold of the Air Fryer place, the eggplants varnished with olive oil.

3. Spread a sheet of bread with the aioli and add the eggplants.

4. Add the olive oil with the parsley in another layer.

Close the sandwich and Serve up.

Shrimp Sandwiches

Ready in about 15 min | Servings 4 | Easy

Ingredients:

- 1 and ¼ cups of cheddar, shredded
- 6 ounces of canned tiny shrimp, drained
- 3 tablespoons of mayonnaise
- 2 tablespoons of green onions, chopped
- 4 whole-wheat bread slices
- 2 tablespoons of butter, soft

Directions:

1. Mix shrimp and cheese, green onion, and mayo in a cup, then mix well.

2. Place this over half of the slices of bread, cover with the other slices of bread, diagonally split into halves, and sprinkle butter over them.

3. Place the sandwiches in the Air Fryer and cook for 5 minutes at 350° F.

4. When the timer reaches 0, then press the cancel button

5. Split shrimp on sandwiches and serve.

Enjoy!

Mozzarella Spinach Rolls

Ready in about 25 min | Servings 2 | Normal

Ingredients:

- 10½ ounces of spinach leaves, boiled
- 1 tablespoon of grated mozzarella cheese
- 2 tablespoons of breadcrumbs
- 1 onion, finely chopped
- 1clove of garlic, grated
- 1 tablespoon of vegetable oil
- 1 teaspoon of ground red chili
- Salt to taste
- 2 tablespoons of corn flour

Directions:

1. Mash the spinach to make a puree; add the mozzarella, breadcrumbs, garlic, corn flour, and salt. Mix thoroughly and mold into small balls.

2. Mix the onions and red chili with some cheese and mold them into smallerballs. Make a hole into the spinach rolls and insert the cheese rolls into each one. Ensure the rolls are evenly covered on all sides.

3. Brush the rolls with oil and place them in an Air Fryer at 390° F. Cook for about 15 minutes until crisp, and serve with a tomato sauce.

Crispy Eggplant Strips

Ready in about 30 min | Servings 2 | Normal

Ingredients:

- 4 tablespoons of cornstarch
- 1 medium-sized eggplant
- 4 tablespoons of vegetable oil
- 1 pinch of salt
- 4 tablespoons of water

Directions:

1. Select bake mode the set the temperature to heat your Air Fryer to 390°F.
2. Slice the eggplant into 0.3 x 3 inches strips.
3. Mix the oil, cornstarch, and water in a bowl. Add the eggplant strips and mix to coat evenly.
4. Put half of the eggplant strips in the Air Fryer and cook for about 14 minutes until they begin to brown. Do the same to the next batch of eggplant strips until they are all cooked.
5. Serve while hot with a yogurt dip.

Crisp Parmesan-Potato Balls

Ready in about 25 min | Servings 4 | Normal

Ingredients:

For the Filling:

- 8 ounces of Parmesan, grated
- 2 egg yolks
- 6 teaspoons of flour
- A pinch of nutmeg
- 4 medium-sized potatoes, peeled and chopped
- 1½ ounce of chopped chives
- A pinch of ground black pepper
- A pinch of salt

For the Breading:

- 6 ounces of breadcrumbs
- 6 ounces of flour
- 2 eggs, whisked
- 3 tablespoons of olive oil

Directions:

1. Cook the potatoes in water with a little salt for about 15 minutes and drain.
2. Use a potato masher to mash the potatoes to form a pulped mass and allow it to cool.
3. Add the parmesan, egg yolk, chives, and flour and mix thoroughly. Add the salt, nutmeg, and pepper. Roll the potato fillings into small round balls.
4. Select bake mode the set the temperature to heat your Air Fryer to 390°F.
5. Add the oil to the breadcrumbs and mix with finger tips until it become scrumbly.

6. Roll the balls over the flour, dip into the whisked eggs, and lastly, coat with the breadcrumbs. Press to ensure coating sticks firmly.

7. Put the potato balls into the basket and Air Fry until golden for about 8 minutes.

Enjoy!

Sweet Potato and Parsnips Crisps

Ready in about 25 min | Servings 2 | Normal

Ingredients:

- 1 medium-sized sweet potato, peeled
- 2 medium-sized beets
- 2 medium-sized parsnips
- ½ teaspoon of ground chili
- 3 teaspoons of vegetable oil

Directions:

1. Select bake mode the set the temperature to preheat your Air Fryer to 460°F.
2. Cut the beets, potato, and parsnips into thin slices. Add the oil, chili, salt, and pepper, and then toss to mix.
3. Put into Air Fryer and cook for 10 minutes. Shake the pan and continue cooking until crisp and golden for another 10 minutes.
4. Serve and Enjoy.

Potatoes Au Gratin

Ready in about 45 min | Servings 6 | Normal

Ingredients:

- 7 medium russet potatoes, peeled and sliced wafer-thin
- ½ cup of cream
- ½ cup of milk
- 1 teaspoon of black pepper
- ½ teaspoon of nutmeg
- ½ cup of gruyere, grated

Directions:

1. Select bake mode the set the temperature to preheat the Air Fryer to 390°F. Combine cream and milk in a bowl and then season with nutmeg, pepper, and salt to taste.

2. Coat the thinly sliced potato with the milk mixture and then remove it to a baking dish.

3. Pour the remaining cream mixture on top of the potatoes. Put the baking dish in the cooking basket into the Air Fryer. Cook for 25 minutes and then remove it.

4. Distribute the cheese uniformly over the potatoes. Bake for 10 minutes until brown.

Air fried Kale Chips

Ready in about 9 min | Servings 1-2 | Normal

Ingredients:

- 1 head of kale
- 1 tablespoon of olive oil
- 1 teaspoon of soya sauce

Directions:

1. Take out the center steam of the kale and tear it up into 1 1/2 pieces. Wash the pieces and dry well.

2. Next, toss with the soya sauce and olive oil. Place in the Air Fryer at 400° F for 2 to 3 minutes, tossing halfway through. Enjoy!

Air-Fried Calamari

Ready in about 20 min | Servings 2 | Normal

Ingredients:

- 1 1/2 pounds of baby squid, cut hoods into rings, and separate tentacles.
- 5-6 cups + 2 tablespoons of vegetable oil
- 1/2 cup of semolina flour
- 1/2 cup of all-purpose flour
- 1/2 teaspoon of old Bay seasoning
- 1/3 cup of plain cornmeal
- ½ teaspoon of black salt pepper, to the taste

Directions:

1. Rinse squid well in cold water. Cut off the tentacles using one cut but keep1/4 an inch of the hood to keep all the tentacles in one piece. For larger squid, make them bite-sized by cutting pieces in half lengthwise.
2. Add oil to a medium-sized deep pot; the oil must reach 4 inches up the side of the pot. Heat the oil to 325° F. In the meantime, combine the dry mixture in a
bowl and set aside.
3. With the oil heated up, dredge your squid. Squeeze off any liquid and dredge the squid in the dry mixture. (Work in batches).
4. Lower the calamari gently into the hot oil and fry back and forth. Remove after 2 to 1/2 minutes or golden brown. Drain on a paper-towel-lined plate (work in batches).
5. Serve with marinara sauce and lemon wedges on the side.

Cheddar Bacon Croquettes

Ready in about 50 min | Servings 4 | Normal

Ingredients:

For the Filling:

- 1-poundof bacon, sliced thinly and set at room temperature
- 1-poundof sharp cheddar cheese, block (cut into 6 portions of 1-inch x 1¾-inch each)

For the Breading:

- 1 cup of all-purpose flour
- 4 tablespoons of olive oil
- 1 cup of seasoned breadcrumbs

Directions:

1. Wrap 2 bacon pieces around each cheddar piece completely. Trim off any fat excess, freeze the cheddar bacon bites for 5 minutes to make firm, but not to freeze.
2. Preheat Air Fryer to 390° F. Combine the breadcrumbs and oil and stir until it becomes loose and crumbly.
3. Put the cheddar block into the flour, place the eggs, and then finally the breadcrumbs, pressing the coating to the croquettes to make sure it sticks.
4. To prevent cheese from running out, double the coating by dipping twice into the egg and then the breadcrumbs
5. Place the croquettes in the basket and cook until golden brown or for about 8 minutes.

Moroccan Meatballs with Mint Yogurt

Ready in about 35 min | Servings 4 | Normal

Ingredients:

For the Meatballs

- 1 egg white
- 4 ounces of ground turkey
- 1-poundof ground lamb
- 1 tablespoon of mint, finely chopped
- 1½ tablespoons of parsley, finely chopped
- 1teaspoon of ground cumin
- 1 teaspoon of cayenne pepper
- 1 teaspoon of ground coriander
- 1 teaspoon of red chili paste
- ¼ cup of olive oil
- 2 garlic cloves, finely chopped
- 1 teaspoon of salt

For the Mint Yogurt:

- ¼ cup of sour cream
- ½ cup of non-Fat: Greek yogurt
- ¼ cup of mint, finely chopped
- 2 tablespoons of buttermilk
- 1 garlic clove, finely chopped
- 2 pinches of salt

Directions:

1. Select bake mode the set the temperature to preheat the Air Fryer to 390°F. In a large mixing bowl, add all the meatball ingredients.

2. Roll the meatballs between your hands until it is as small as a golf ball. Place the rolled meatballs into the cooking basket and set the timer for 6 to 8 minutes.

3. Meanwhile, combine all the mint yogurt ingredients to a medium mixing bowl, mixing well 4. Garnish the meatballs with fresh mint and olive and enjoy.

Tomato, Cheese 'n Broccoli Quiche

Ready about in: 24 min| Serves 2|

Ingredients

- ½ cup Cheddar Cheese grated
- ½ cup Whole Milk
- 1 Large Carrot, peeled and diced
- 1 Large Tomato, chopped
- 1 small Broccoli, cut into florets
- 1 teaspoons Parsley
- 1 teaspoons Thyme
- 2 Large Eggs
- 2 teaspoons Feta Cheese
- Salt & Pepper

Directions:

1. Lightly grease baking pan of Air Fryer with cooking spray.
2. Spread carrots, broccoli, and tomato in baking pan.
3. For 10 minutes, cook on 330° F.
4. Meanwhile, in a medium bowl whisk well eggs and milk. Season generously with pepper and salt. Whisk in parsley and thyme.
5. Remove basket and toss the mixture a bit. Sprinkle cheddar cheese. Pour egg mixture over vegetables and cheese.
6. Cook for another 12 minutes or until set to desired doneness.
7. Sprinkle feta cheese and let it sit for 2 minutes.
8. Serve and enjoy.

Tasty Hash Brown

Ready in about 30 mins | Serving 6 | Easy

Ingredients:

- 16 ounces of hash browns
- ¼ cup of olive oil
- ½ teaspoon of paprika
- ½ teaspoon of garlic powder
- Salt and black pepper to the taste
- 1 egg, whisked
- 2 tablespoon of chives, chopped
- 1 cup of cheddar, shredded

Directions:

1. Apply the oil to the Air Fryer, pump it up to 350° F, and apply brown hash.
2. Remove the paprika, garlic powder, salt, pepper, and egg, mix for 15 minutes, and fry.
3. Add the cheddar and chives, toss, break and serve between plates. Enjoy!

Pork Barbecue Sandwich

Ready in about 1hr 55 min | Servings 4 | Difficult

Ingredients:

- Two slices of white bread
- 1 tbsp of softened butter
- 1/2 lbs of cut pork (in cubes)
- 1 little capsicum
- For sauce barbeque:
- 1/4 tablespoons of Worcestershire
- 1/2 tablespoons of olive oil
- 1/2 crushed garlic flake
- 1/4 cup of onion
- 1/4 tablespoons of powder mustard
- 1/2 tablespoons of sugar
- 1/4 tablespoons of hot chili sauce
- 1 tablespoons of tomatoes ketchup
- 1/2 cup of water.
- A pinch of salt and black chilies to the taste

Directions:

1. Take the bread slices and cut the rims. Now clean the slices in the horizontal way. Heat the sauce ingredients and wait before sauce thickens.

2. Now fill in the pork into the sauce before it gets its flavors. Stir in the capsicum and Peel off skin. The capsicum is sliced into strips. Combine products. And add it to slices of bread.

3. Select bake mode the set the temperature to preheat the Air Fryer to 300°F for 5 minutes. Open the Fryer basket and put the sandwiches prepared in it so that no 2 Sandwiches bump into each other. Now hold the fryer at 250° F for Fifteen minutes.

4. When the timer reaches 0, then press the cancel button

5. Turn the sandwiches in between the cooking to Cook slices of both. Serve the sandwiches with tomato ketchup or chutney.

Fish Club Sandwich

Ready in about 30 min | Servings 2 | Normal

Ingredients:

- 2 slices of white bread
- 1 tablespoons of softened butter
- 1 tin of tuna
- 1 small capsicum

For Barbeque Sauce:

- ¼ tablespoons of Worcestershire sauce
- ½ tablespoons of olive oil
- ½ flake of garlic crushed
- ¼ cup of chopped onion
- ¼ tablespoons of mustard powder
- ½ tablespoons of sugar
- ¼ tablespoons. of red chili sauce
- 1 tablespoons of tomato ketchup
- ½ cup of water.
- **A pinch of salt and black pepper to taste**

Directions:

1. Take the bread slices and cut the rims. Still cut horizontally on the strips. Heat the sauce ingredients and wait before sauce thickens. Now add the fish to the sauce and whisk before the flavors are acquired.

2. Whisk the capsicum and scrape off the flesh. The capsicum is sliced into strips. Mix the ingredients, and add them to the slices of bread.

3. Preheat the Air Fryer to 300° F for 5 minutes. Open the Fryer's basket and put the cooked sandwiches in it, ensuring that no two sandwiches meet each other.

4. Hold the fryer at about 15 minutes now at 250°. Switch the sandwiches to cook both slices in between the cooking process. Serve the strawberry ketchup or mint chutney sandwiches.

Air Fryer Sandwich

Ready in about 16 mins | Serving 2 | Easy

Ingredients:

- 2 English muffins halved
- 2 eggs
- 2 bacon strips
- Salt and black pepper to the taste

Directions:

1. Crack eggs in your Air Fryer, put bacon on top, cover, and cook at 392°F for 6 minutes.

2. Warm up the English muffin halves in the microwave for a few seconds, split eggs into two halves, place bacon on top, sprinkle salt and pepper, cover with the other two English muffins and serve.

Enjoy!

Cheese Sandwich

Ready in about 18 min | Servings 1 | Easy

Ingredients:

- 2 bread slices
- 2 teaspoons of butter
- 2 pieces of cheddar cheese
- A pinch of sweet paprika

Directions:

1. Place the butter on slices of bread, add the cheddar cheese on one, sprinkle the paprika, cover with the other slices of bread, break into 2 halves, put them in the Air Fryer, and cook for 8 minutes at 370° F, turn them once, put them on a plate and serve.

Enjoy!

Onion Flowers

Ready in about 40 min | Servings 6 | Normal

Ingredients:

- 4 medium-sized onions, peeled
- 4 teaspoons of butter
- 3 teaspoons of vegetable oil

Directions:

1. Cut off the bottom and top of the onions. Cut 4 slits into the onions but not through to the end to make 8 segments.

2. Place the onions in salt water for 4 hours to remove the sharp tang.

3. Heat your Air Fryer to 356° F.

4. Place the blooming onions in the fryer basket. Add a teaspoon of butter oneach and drizzle with oil—Cook for 30 minutes.

5. Remove the charred outer layer and serve.

Sweet Pepper and Potato Stuffed Bread Rolls

Ready in about 20 min | Servings 3 | Normal

Ingredients:

- 6 medium-sized potatoes, boiled
- 2 teaspoons of flour
- 6 slices of white bread
- 1 tablespoon of sesame seed
- 1 pound of chopped bell peppers (red and green)
- ½ teaspoon of chat masala seasoning
- Salt to taste

Directions:

1. Mash the cooked potatoes in a large bowl and add the seasoning and salt. Stir thoroughly.
2. Add water to the flour to make a thick slurry mixture. Mix sesame seeds and the chopped pepper in a separate bowl.
3. Peel off the brown edges of the bread and use a rolling pin to flatten it. Put the potato stuffing on the edge of the bread and roll it into a cylinder.
4. Seal the rolls by brushing the edge with the flour mixture. Use the mixture to coat the rolls as well. Place the rolls in the mixture of pepper and sesame seeds and allow to coat.
5. Heat your Air Fryer to 330° F and place the rolls in it. Bake for 5 minutes and remove it. Serve hot with ketchup.

Crispy Parsley and Garlic Mushrooms

Ready in about 20 min | Servings 4 | Normal

Ingredients:

- 2 slices of white bread
- 3 teaspoons of finely chopped parsley
- 16 small mushrooms
- 4 teaspoons of melted butter
- 1 clove of garlic, crushed
- ½ teaspoon of black pepper

Directions:

1. Heat your Air Fryer to 390°F.

2. When the timer reaches 0, then press the cancel button

3. Grind the bread using a food processor into fine crumbs. Add the parsley, garlic, and pepper and mix thoroughly. Add the melted butter and stir.

4. Remove all the mushroom stalks and Put the breadcrumbs into the caps. Press to keep breadcrumbs firm in the cap.

5. Put the caps into the fryer basket and cook for 8 minutes until they become crisp and golden brown.

Crispy Broccoli Tots

Ready in about 50 min | Servings 4 | Normal

Ingredients:

- 2 cups of broccoli florets
- 1¼ cup of white cheddar cheese
- 1¼ cup of panko crumbs
- 1/4 cup of parmesan cheese
- 2 eggs, beaten
- 1 teaspoon of kosher salt

Directions:

1. Pulse broccoli with a food processor until finely crumbed.

2. Combine broccoli, cheeses, panko crumbs, and salt in a large bowl. Add eggs and mix thoroughly.

3. Roll mixture into small balls and refrigerate for 30 minutes to firm— Preheat Air Fryer to 350°F.

4. Place the broccoli tots into the Air Fryer and then cook until browned and crispy for 12 minutes. Remove and serve.

Roasted Winter Vegetables

Ready in about 25 min | Servings 6 | Normal

Ingredients:

- 2 red onions, cut into wedges
- 1 1/3 cup of parsnips, peeled and cut into 2 cm cubes
- 1 1/3 cup of butternut squash, halved, seeded, and cubed
- 1 1/3 cup of celery, peeled and cut into 2 cm cubes
- 1 tablespoon of fresh thyme needles
- 1 tablespoon of olive oil, pepper, and salt

Directions:

1. Select bake mode the set the temperature to preheat the Air Fryer to 390° F.
2. Combine the cut vegetables with the olive oil and thyme and season well to taste.
3. Place the veggies into the basket and place the basket into the Air Fryer.
4. Roast the vegetables for 20 minutes, stirring once until brown and done.

Cheesy Polenta

Ready in about 1hr 5mins | Servings 6 | Difficult

Ingredients:

- 2 ½ cups of cooked polenta
- 1 cup of marinara sauce
- 1/4 cup of parmesan, shaved
- 1 tablespoon of vegetable oil
- Salt to taste

Directions

1. Grease a baking tray with vegetable oil. Place the polenta into the tray and then refrigerate for 1 hour to firm.

2. Select bake mode the set the temperature to preheat the Air Fryer to 350°F. Remove the tray from the fridge and cut the polenta into equal slices.

3. Place the slices into the Air Fryer and cook minutes until crispy or for 5-6 minutes.

4. Sprinkle with parmesan, season with salt, and serve with marinara on the side.

Cajun Shrimp

Ready in about 10 min | Servings 4 | Normal

Ingredients:

- 1¼ pounds of tiger shrimp
- ¼ teaspoon of smoked paprika
- ½ teaspoon of old bay seasoning
- ¼ teaspoon of cayenne pepper
- 1 tablespoon of olive oil
- 1 pinch of salt

Directions:

1. Select bake mode the set the temperature to preheat the Air Fryer to 390°F. Combine all ingredients in a mixing bowl; let the shrimp coat well with the oil and spices.

2. Place the shrimp into the cooking basket in the Air Fryer and cook for 5 minutes.

3. When the timer reaches 0, then press the cancel button

4.. Serve with rice and enjoy.

Broccoli Rounds with Cheese

Ready in about 2hrs25 min | Servings 6 | Normal

Ingredients

- 16-ounce Broccoli, chopped
- 3 cups of cheddar cheese, shredded
- 3 eggs
- 1 cup of flour
- 1 cup of breadcrumbs
- Salt and pepper to taste

Directions

1. Whisk the eggs in a bowl and then add the broccoli, cheese, and flour to make a dough. Cover and then put inside the refrigerator for at least 2 hours.
2. Use a spoonful of the mixture to compress into balls, then roll into the breadcrumbs to coat.
3. Select bake mode the set the temperature to preheat the Air Fryer to 350° F. Fry the broccoli rounds in batches for 4 to 5 minutes.
4. When the timer reaches 0, then press the cancel button
5. Serve with ranch dip and enjoy.

Coconut Chicken Bites

Ready in about 25 min | Servings 4 | Normal

Ingredients:

- 2 teaspoons of garlic powder
- 2 eggs
- Salt and black pepper to the taste
- ¾ cup of panko bread crumbs
- ¾ cup of coconut, shredded
- Cooking spray
- 8 chicken tenders

Directions:

1. Mix the eggs with salt, pepper, and garlic powder in a cup, then whisk well.
2. Mix coconut and panko in another dish, then mix well.
3. Mix the chicken tenders into the shells and roll one well in the coconut.
4. Sprinkle chicken bits with cooking oil, bring them in the Air Fryers bowl, and cook for 10 minutes at 350° F.
5. Put them up on a tray, and act as an appetizer.

Enjoy!

Cauliflower Snack

Ready in about 25 min | Servings 4 | Normal

Ingredients:

- 4 cups of cauliflower florets
- 1 cup of panko bread crumbs
- ¼ cup of butter, melted
- ¼ cup of buffalo sauce
- Mayonnaise for serving

Directions:

1. Mix butter and buffalo sauce in a tub, then shake well.

2. In this combination, roll the cauliflower florets and cover them in crumbs of panko crust.

3. Place these in the basket of your Air Fryer and cook for 15 minutes at 350° F.

4. Arrange them on a pan, then serve side by side with mayo.

Enjoy!

Sausage Balls

Ready in about 25 min | Servings 9 | Normal

Ingredients:

- 4 ounces of sausage meat, ground
- Salt and black pepper to the taste
- 1 teaspoon of sage
- ½ teaspoon of garlic, minced
- 1 small onion, chopped
- 3 tablespoons of breadcrumbs

Directions:

1. In a bowl, mix sausage with salt, pepper, sage, garlic, onion, and breadcrumbs, stir well and shape small balls out of this mix.

2. Put them in your Air Fryer's basket, cook at 360° F for 15 minutes, divide into bowls

3. When the timer reaches 0, then press the cancel button

4. serve as a snack.

Enjoy!

Chicken Dip

Ready in about 35 min | Servings 10 | Normal

Ingredients:

- 3 tablespoons of butter, melted
- 1 cup of yogurt
- 12 ounces of cream cheese
- 2 cups of chicken meat, cooked and shredded
- 2 teaspoons of curry powder
- 4 scallions, chopped
- 6 ounces of Monterey jack cheese, grated
- 1/3 cup of raisins
- ¼ cup of cilantro, chopped
- ½ cup of almonds, sliced
- Salt and black pepper to the taste
- ½ cup of chutney

Directions:

1. In a bowl, mix cream cheese with yogurt and whisk using your mixer.
2. Add curry powder, scallions, chicken meat, raisins, cheese, cilantro, salt, and pepper and stir everything.
3. Spread this into a baking dish that fist your Air Fryer, sprinkle almonds on top, place in your Air Fryer, bake at 300° for 25 minutes, divide into bowls, top with chutney, and serve as an appetizer.
Enjoy!

Sweet Popcorn

Ready in about 25 min | Servings 4 | Normal

Ingredients:

- 2 tablespoons of corn kernels
- 2 and ½ tablespoons of butter
- 2 ounces of brown sugar

Directions:

1. Place the corn kernels in the pan of your Air Fryer, cook them for 6 minutes at 400° F, move them to a plate, spread them out, and set them aside for now.

2. Heat a casserole over low pressure, add butter, melt it, add sugar, and whisk before dissolving.

3. Attach popcorn, throw to cover, heat off and scatter over the tray again.

4. Refrigerate, break into bowls, and serve as a snack.

Enjoy!

Squash Fritters

Ready in about 17 min | Servings 4 | Easy

Ingredients:

- 3 ounces of cream cheese
- 1 egg, whisked
- ½ teaspoon of oregano, dried
- A pinch of salt and black pepper
- 1 yellow summer squash, grated
- 1/3 cup of carrot, grated
- 2/3 cup of bread crumbs
- 2 tablespoons of olive oil

Directions:

1. In a bowl, mix cream cheese with salt, pepper, oregano, egg, breadcrumbs, carrot, and squash and stir well.
2. Shape medium patties out of this mix and brush them with the oil.
3. Place squash patties in your Air Fryer and cook them at 400° F for 7 minutes.
4. When the timer reaches 0, then press the cancel button
5. Serve them

Enjoy!

Cauliflower Buffalo

Ready in about 15 min | Servings 2 | Normal

Ingredients

- 4 cups of cauliflower florets
- 2 spoonful of salted butter, melted
- 1/2 (1-ounce) package of fresh ranch seasoning
- 1/4 cup of buffalo sauce

Directions:

1. Sprinkle the cauliflower with butter in a wide bowl and dry. Put the basket into the Air Fryer.

2. Adjust the temperature and set the timer to 400° F For 5 minutes.

3. When preparing, shake the basket 2 or 3 times. Drop cauliflower from the fryer basket when tender and sprinkle with buffalo sauce. Serve hot.

Fries Avocado

Ready in about 15 min | Servings 2 | Normal

Ingredients

- 2 Medium advocates
- 1 ounce of pork rinds, finely soiled

Directions:

1. Cut out half of each avocado. Have the pit removed and cut the flesh into 1/4"-thick slices.

2. In a medium bowl, place the pork rinds and press each slice of avocado coated in the pork rinds. Place the pieces of avocado in the Air Fryer basket.

3. Change the temperature to 350° F and timer configuration to 5 minutes.

4. Immediately serve.

Coco Milk and Paprika Drumstick

Ready about in: 30 min| Serves 6|

Ingredients

- ½ cup almond flour
- ½ cup coconut milk
- ½ teaspoon oregano
- ½ teaspoon paprika
- ½ teaspoon salt
- 3 tablespoons melted butter
- 6 chicken drumsticks

Instructions

1. Select bake mode the set the temperature to Preheat the Air Fryer for 5 minutes.
2. Soak the chicken drumsticks in coconut milk.
3. In a mixing bowl, combine the almond flour, salt, paprika, and oregano.
4. Dredge the chicken in the almond flour mixture.
5. Place the chicken pieces in the air fryer basket.
6. Air Fry for 30 minutes at 325° F.
7. Halfway through the Cooking Time, give the fryer basket a shape.
8. Drizzle with melted butter once cooked.

www.ingramcontent.com/pod-product-compliance
Lightning Source LLC
Chambersburg PA
CBHW070911080526
44589CB00013B/1262